SACRED SPACE

Also by the Irish Jesuits

Sacred Space: The Prayer Book

SACRED SPACE

A LITTLE BOOK OF ENCOURAGEMENT

Adapted from **SACRED SPACE**, founded by the IRISH JESUITS

Edited by VINITA HAMPTON WRIGHT

LOYOLA PRESS.
A JESUIT MINISTRY
Chicago

LOYOLA PRESS.
A JESUIT MINISTRY

3441 N. Ashland Avenue
Chicago, Illinois 60657
(800) 621-1008
www.loyolapress.com

Scripture quotations are from the *New Revised Standard Version Bible: Catholic Edition*, copyright 1989, 1993, Division of Christian Education of the National Council of the Churches of Christ in the United States of America. Used by permission. All rights reserved.

Cover art credit: ©iStock.com/MalyDesigner, ©iStock.com/ekmelica, ©iStock.com/oopoontongoo, yuelan/iStock/Thinkstock

ISBN-13: 978-0-8294-4497-1
ISBN-10: 0-8294-4497-1
Library of Congress Control Number: 9780829444971

Printed in the United States of America.
17 18 19 20 21 22 23 Versa 10 9 8 7 6 5 4 3 2 1

Contents

How to Use This Book

We have chosen material from the Sacred Space website that focuses on the need we all have for encouragement in a variety of situations. There are seventy short chapters; each includes a Gospel reading, a short reflection, and a prayer. Each entry is given a descriptive title.

To use this little book, simply look through the table of contents and choose a title that speaks to you. Spend time with the Gospel reading, then use the reflection as a starting point for your own meditation. End with the prayer provided, with your own words, or with a standard prayer such as the Our Father.

Through his actions and teachings, Jesus demonstrated how we might live in a way that brings the kingdom of God into daily experience. But he also revealed a way of seeing: a mind-set of hope to offset this world's many troubles and dangers. He told his followers then—and he tells us now—to believe in God, to not be afraid, to love one another, and to receive the many benefits of God's care and compassion.

Jesus did not promise that we would escape hard times or be immune to the turbulent emotions that accompany loss, betrayal, poverty, guilt, or persecution. He did promise that God's love would provide for us, comfort us, and show us the way through the turbulence.

We hope that these scenes from Jesus' journey through human life will touch your own life where it hurts or where it has grown weary, angry, or confused. To prepare for each reading, you might try this simple sequence, or some version of it:

- Take a moment to be present to God. Be still and imagine God's loving gaze upon you. Open your life to that love.

- Allow other thoughts and distractions to move through your mind but then place them off to the side during this time of prayer and meditation.

- Ask the Holy Spirit to prepare your heart and mind for the Scripture you're about to read. Ask for understanding and for the ability to see clearly what God wants to show you.

- Thank God for this moment in time and for this opportunity to be encouraged.

Are we often weary, disheartened, and sad? Do we think that we won't be able to cope? Let us not close our hearts, let us not lose confidence, let us never give up. There are no situations that God cannot change; there is no sin that he cannot forgive if only we open ourselves to him.
—Pope Francis, *The Church of Mercy*

1

Don't Give Up Praying to God

Jesus told them a parable about their need to pray always and not to lose heart. . . . "In a certain city there was a judge who neither feared God nor had respect for people. In that city there was a widow who kept coming to him and saying, 'Grant me justice against my opponent.' For a while he refused; but later he said to himself, 'Though I have no fear of God and no respect for anyone, yet because this widow keeps bothering me, I will grant her justice.' . . . Listen to what the unjust judge says. And will not God grant justice to his chosen ones who cry to him day and night?"

—Luke 18:1–7

Reflect

We can model our prayer after that of the widow in Jesus' parable. Her persistence does not falter. In prayer I can present my true self to God. God knows the real me anyway, and he is a God of justice. Do I really believe this? Do I pray and work for justice in the situations around me? Is there something I'm praying for fiercely like the widow?

Pray

Lord, please wake up, within me, the fierce desire to do what's right and to ask for what this world needs. Help me be as persistent as the widow in this story. You show me through her example that persistence is as much about hope as it is about stubbornness. Yes, I want to be stubbornly hopeful!

Mary's Vision of God's Desire for Us

And Mary said,
"My soul magnifies the Lord,
and my spirit rejoices in God my Savior,
for he has looked with favor on the lowliness of his servant.
Surely, from now on all generations will call me blessed;
for the Mighty One has done great things for me,
and holy is his name.
His mercy is for those who fear him
from generation to generation.
He has shown strength with his arm;
he has scattered the proud in the thoughts of their hearts.
He has brought down the powerful from their thrones,
and lifted up the lowly;
he has filled the hungry with good things,
and sent the rich away empty.
He has helped his servant Israel,
in remembrance of his mercy,
according to the promise he made to our ancestors,
to Abraham and to his descendants forever."
And Mary remained with her for about three months and
then returned to her home.

—Luke 1:46–56

Reflect

This glorious prayer, the Magnificat, is charged like dynamite. It points to a society in which nobody wants to have too much while others have too little. The hungry are fed and the lowly are raised up. How do I nurture this world in my own heart? How can I nurture it in my daily life? How do I say "Yes" to God's desire for me as Mary did?

Pray

Lord, give me Mary's confidence and generosity of spirit. I ask not only to listen to your voice and do your will but also to do these things joyfully and fearlessly. Let me answer your call with an exultant "Yes!" because I know that my journey into the unknown will be made radiant by your transfiguring presence.

When It's Time to Get Away

The apostles gathered around Jesus, and told him all that they had done and taught. He said to them, "Come away to a deserted place all by yourselves and rest a while." For many were coming and going, and they had no leisure even to eat.

And they went away in the boat to a deserted place by themselves. Now many saw them going and recognized them, and they hurried there on foot from all the towns and arrived ahead of them. As he went ashore, he saw a great crowd; and he had compassion for them, because they were like sheep without a shepherd; and he began to teach them many things.

—Mark 6:30–34

Reflect

The apostles were concerned about their tasks of ministry. Jesus seems to say to them, "Stand back a little. Perhaps it's not all about you but about what God is doing in and through you." In what subtle ways is God acting in my life right now? Am I in need of rest and reflection too?

Pray

Jesus, help me understand when it's time to get away for rest and for a refreshed perspective.

Am I Obsessed with Things?

"Do not store up for yourselves treasures on earth, where moth and rust consume and where thieves break in and steal; but store up for yourselves treasures in heaven, where neither moth nor rust consumes and where thieves do not break in and steal. For where your treasure is, there your heart will be also.

"The eye is the lamp of the body. So, if your eye is healthy, your whole body will be full of light; but if your eye is unhealthy, your whole body will be full of darkness. If then the light in you is darkness, how great is the darkness!"

—Matthew 6:19–23

Reflect

Jesus invites his hearers to a deeper level of understanding by contrasting earthly treasures with heavenly ones and darkness with light. Have I something to learn here? Do I hold too tightly to my things? Do I find myself obsessing over what I could have? What would Jesus say to me about these treasures? Are they holding me back from a closer relationship with Jesus? Or from what he is calling me to do?

Pray

Lord, I've become too concerned with treasures that don't last. My life seems to revolve around tasks and things. Thank you for giving me permission to lessen the importance of "things" in my life. Thank you for reminding me to focus on heavenly treasures such as faith, compassion, hope, and spiritual freedom.

5

Safe in God's Hands

"My sheep hear my voice. I know them, and they follow me. I give them eternal life, and they will never perish. No one will snatch them out of my hand. What my Father has given me is greater than all else, and no one can snatch it out of the Father's hand. The Father and I are one."

—John 10:27–30

Reflect

Those who identify with Jesus hear his voice and come to know and trust in him. They follow in love, wanting only to be in relationship with him. It is God's gift to me that I can recognize Jesus' voice and choose to follow him. What does it mean to me to know that no one can take me out of God's hands? And that I am promised eternal life? I imagine myself resting in God's hand, letting his peace and radiant love pour over me. As I rest, I recognize Jesus' voice, calling me to follow him, telling me I'm safe.

Pray

Lord, thank you for always knowing me. I am forever held in your hands in a deep and intimate relationship. I pray for those people who, suffering illness such as dementia, no longer recognize the ones they loved, and I pray for those who care for them. Be their Good Shepherd in their valley of darkness.

6

When I Feel Unseen and Insignificant

Soon afterwards he went on through cities and villages,
proclaiming and bringing the good news of the kingdom of
God. The twelve were with him, as well as some women who
had been cured of evil spirits and infirmities: Mary, called
Magdalene, from whom seven demons had gone out, and
Joanna, the wife of Herod's steward Chuza, and Susanna, and
many others, who provided for them out of their resources.

—Luke 8:1–3

Reflect

We know little about Susanna and Joanna other than that they were happy to follow Jesus and were recognized by Luke as disciples. Just think of all those quiet disciples whose lives and prayers have contributed to the church but who have left little evident legacy. Who do I know who's living a quiet but influential life? And do I ever feel that my own efforts are overlooked or insignificant?

Pray

God, for all—especially women—who support others through their presence, help them draw encouragement from knowing that Jesus sees, recognizes, and loves their passionate service. I include myself in this prayer today, because sometimes I feel invisible and unimportant.

7

Sometimes the Temple
Needs Cleaning

Then he entered the temple and began to drive out those who
were selling things there; and he said, "It is written,

'My house shall be a house of prayer';
but you have made it a den of robbers."

Every day he was teaching in the temple. The chief priests,
the scribes, and the leaders of the people kept looking for a
way to kill him; but they did not find anything they could
do, for all the people were spellbound by what they heard.

—Luke 19:45–48

Reflect

The templegoers seem not to have noticed what the hucksters had done to the holy place as they changed money and sold animals for sacrifice. Commerce tends to grow and grow when it finds a market, so the temple, the place of prayer, had degenerated into a sort of marketplace. Jesus needed to challenge that drift and reassert the place's holiness. His anger was appropriate and expressed God's desires. Do I ever feel as if I'm consumed by this endless hunger for more—more money, more possessions? Do I find myself hungering for God's grace?

Pray

Lord, you desire to dwell in this temple that is my body, but the pressure to survive, and then the appetite for more money, can so possess me that I find little space for you. Please make my soul a place of prayer.

8

In Need of a Larger Heart

As Jesus was walking along, he saw a man called Matthew
sitting at the tax booth; and he said to him, "Follow me." And
he got up and followed him.

And as he sat at dinner in the house, many tax collectors and
sinners came and were sitting with him and his disciples.
When the Pharisees saw this, they said to his disciples, "Why
does your teacher eat with tax collectors and sinners?" But
when he heard this, he said, "Those who are well have no
need of a physician, but those who are sick. Go and learn
what this means, 'I desire mercy, not sacrifice.' For I have
come to call not the righteous but sinners."

—Matthew 9:9–13

Reflect

Jesus is inclusive—even "tax-collectors and sinners" are welcomed. They represent those whose professions and social status are not "respectable." But Jesus shows that he has come for all people, without exception, and especially for the weak and the vulnerable, the sick and the sinners. Can I feel Jesus' love for me too? Regardless of what I've done? And can I see his mercy at work around me?

Pray

First of all, Jesus, have I believed and accepted that your love includes me—no matter what I've done or thought or said, or how my life may have digressed from the life you want for me? Second, am I prejudiced against any individuals or groups? Lord, help me become more like you in thought, word, and deed. Make me largehearted.

9

Am I Afraid to Surrender?

Very truly, I tell you, unless a grain of wheat falls into the earth and dies, it remains just a single grain; but if it dies, it bears much fruit. Those who love their life lose it, and those who hate their life in this world will keep it for eternal life. Whoever serves me must follow me, and where I am, there will my servant be also. Whoever serves me, the Father will honor.

—John 12:24–26

Reflect

God can use us to affect the lives of many people for good. But for this to happen, we need to be following Jesus, not following our own whims and preferences. We need to surrender our lives and ask the question, "Lord, what do you want me to do with my life today?"

Pray

Lord, I'm afraid to die like that grain of wheat—I admit it! Grace me with the gift of letting go of all that I cling to. May I not block your Spirit moving in me. Work through me so that I may carry you to all those whose lives I touch.

10

Jesus Finds Us Weeping

But Mary stood weeping outside the tomb. As she wept, she bent over to look into the tomb; and she saw two angels in white, sitting where the body of Jesus had been lying, one at the head and the other at the feet. They said to her, "Woman, why are you weeping?" She said to them, "They have taken away my Lord, and I do not know where they have laid him." When she had said this, she turned round and saw Jesus standing there, but she did not know that it was Jesus. Jesus said to her, "Woman, why are you weeping? For whom are you looking?" Supposing him to be the gardener, she said to him, "Sir, if you have carried him away, tell me where you have laid him, and I will take him away." Jesus said to her, "Mary!" She turned and said to him in Hebrew, "Rabbouni!" (which means Teacher). Jesus said to her, "Do not hold on to me, because I have not yet ascended to the Father. But go to my brothers and say to them, 'I am ascending to my Father and your Father, to my God and your God.'" Mary Magdalene went and announced to the disciples, "I have seen the Lord"; and she told them that he had said these things to her.

—John 20:11–18

Reflect

Mary Magdalene weeps for what she thinks is missing, her tears making it difficult for her to see who is present. The celebration of Easter not only rescues us from our sin but also calls us beyond our dutiful habits, our worthy projects, and our personal values. Jesus asks us, "Whom are you looking for?" and invites us to let our hopes carry us to meaningful action. He wants to enrich us and help us recognize where his Spirit is moving in our lives.

Pray

Dear Jesus, you don't judge me for times of sorrow, confusion, hurt, and tears. As you met Mary when she wept, not understanding the real situation, so you meet me when I don't know what is happening but do know sorrow and longing. Help me recognize your presence today.

11

Can I Trust God to Hear Me?

And he said to them, "Suppose one of you has a friend, and you go to him at midnight and say to him, 'Friend, lend me three loaves of bread; for a friend of mine has arrived, and I have nothing to set before him.' And he answers from within, 'Do not bother me; the door has already been locked, and my children are with me in bed; I cannot get up and give you anything.' I tell you, even though he will not get up and give him anything because he is his friend, at least because of his persistence he will get up and give him whatever he needs. So I say to you, Ask, and it will be given to you; search, and you will find; knock, and the door will be opened for you. For everyone who asks receives, and everyone who searches finds, and for everyone who knocks, the door will be opened. Is there anyone among you who, if your child asks for a fish, will give a snake instead of a fish? Or if the child asks for an egg, will give a scorpion? If you then, who are evil, know how to give good gifts to your children, how much more will the heavenly Father give the Holy Spirit to those who ask him!"

—Luke 11:5–13

Reflect

There are people whom I would like to be generous to; there may be some whom I would give anything to. Can I imagine that, in God's eyes, *I* am one of those people? God may not seem to give me everything I ask for, but he arranges what is for my good and lasting benefit. As my trust deepens, my prayer becomes not so much anxiety for an answer but a waiting for God with a child's confident trust.

Pray

God, my prayers change as my priorities shift. As I review what is really important, help me identify what I might let go of and what my truest desires are. I want to trust your love. Help me be persistent in my prayers. Help me believe that you hear me.

Jesus Was Praying for Me, Too

"And now I am no longer in the world, but they are in the world, and I am coming to you. Holy Father, protect them in your name that you have given me, so that they may be one, as we are one. While I was with them, I protected them in your name that you have given me. I guarded them, and not one of them was lost except the one destined to be lost, so that the scripture might be fulfilled. But now I am coming to you, and I speak these things in the world so that they may have my joy made complete in themselves. I have given them your word, and the world has hated them because they do not belong to the world, just as I do not belong to the world. I am not asking you to take them out of the world, but I ask you to protect them from the evil one. They do not belong to the world, just as I do not belong to the world. Sanctify them in the truth; your word is truth. As you have sent me into the world, so I have sent them into the world. And for their sakes I sanctify myself, so that they also may be sanctified in truth."

—John 17:11–19

Reflect

Jesus' love for his disciples does not fade. It endures eternally. He asks the Father to protect and guide them. He also entrusts us, his friends and companions, to the loving care of his Father. Notice how he includes us in his desires for mission to the world, protection, holiness, and unity with God. Do I feel part of Jesus' mission, part of his unity with God?

Pray

Remind me, Jesus, that your prayer includes me. And that you continue to pray for me, bringing my life to the Father. You know what is going on in my life, and you understand my responses to stress, fear, opportunity, and grace. You continue to ask that my life be protected from the evil one. Thank you for your enduring care.

13

Am I Facing Temptation?

Jesus, full of the Holy Spirit, returned from the Jordan and was led by the Spirit in the wilderness, where for forty days he was tempted by the devil. He ate nothing at all during those days, and when they were over, he was famished. The devil said to him, "If you are the Son of God, command this stone to become a loaf of bread." Jesus answered him, "It is written,

'One does not live by bread alone.'"

Then the devil led him up and showed him in an instant all the kingdoms of the world. And the devil said to him, "To you I will give their glory and all this authority; for it has been given over to me, and I give it to anyone I please. If you, then, will worship me, it will all be yours." Jesus answered him, "It is written,

'Worship the Lord your God,
and serve only him.'"

Then the devil took him to Jerusalem, and placed him on the pinnacle of the temple, saying to him, "If you are the Son of God, throw yourself down from here, for it is written,

'He will command his angels concerning you,
to protect you,'

and

'On their hands they will bear you up,
so that you will not dash your foot against a stone.'"

Jesus answered him, "It is said, 'Do not put the Lord your God to the test.'" When the devil had finished every test, he departed from him until an opportune time.

—Luke 4:1–13

Reflect

Jesus' experience teaches us that there is nothing wrong with being tempted; it's how we react to the temptation that matters. A short prayer or a quote from God's word will help us let it go. For example, "Lead me not into temptation," or "I must forgive, not once but seventy times." Am I being tempted in my own life right now? Who or what is tempting me? How will I react?

Pray

Lord, you faced real temptation. You had desires—desires for good—that the tempter tried to use against you, and it was truly a struggle for you to resist. Remind me of this when my desires—especially my good desires—become twisted and I risk being drawn away from trust in God and pushed toward what is not best for me.

Do I Really Want to Be Healed?

After this there was a festival of the Jews, and Jesus went
up to Jerusalem.
Now in Jerusalem by the Sheep Gate there is a pool, called in
Hebrew Beth-zatha, which has five porticoes. In these lay
many invalids—blind, lame, and paralyzed. One man was
there who had been ill for thirty-eight years. When Jesus saw
him lying there and knew that he had been there a long time,
he said to him, "Do you want to be made well?" The sick
man answered him, "Sir, I have no one to put me into the
pool when the water is stirred up; and while I am making my
way, someone else steps down ahead of me." Jesus said to
him, "Stand up, take your mat and walk." At once the man
was made well, and he took up his mat and began to walk.
Now that day was a sabbath. So the Jews said to the man who
had been cured, "It is the sabbath; it is not lawful for you to
carry your mat." But he answered them, "The man who made
me well said to me, 'Take up your mat and walk.'" They
asked him, "Who is the man who said to you, 'Take it up and
walk'?" Now the man who had been healed did not know
who it was, for Jesus had disappeared in the crowd that was
there. Later Jesus found him in the temple and said to him,
"See, you have been made well! Do not sin anymore, so that
nothing worse happens to you." The man went away and told

the Jews that it was Jesus who had made him well. Therefore the Jews started persecuting Jesus, because he was doing such things on the sabbath.

—John 5:1–16

Reflect

I can wait all my life for the water to be stirred. How safe it is *not* to see, *not* to have to move! No one can blame me for my inaction because there's nobody to lift me. When Jesus asks, "Do you want to be made well?" I don't really answer the question. I am not sure. If I were healed, then I would have to move on from the familiar place where I've lain all these years. God, stir my heart!

Pray

Dear Jesus, our healer, the man by the pool did not know that you, source of all healing, were standing beside him. Do I look for healing in the wrong places? Do I resist healing because it would require other changes, more responsibilities? Have I alienated people who would help me, if only I'd asked? Help me answer honestly when you ask, "Do you want to be made well?"

15

When Life Seems to Be Over

Soon afterwards he went to a town called Nain, and his disciples and a large crowd went with him. As he approached the gate of the town, a man who had died was being carried out. He was his mother's only son, and she was a widow; and with her was a large crowd from the town. When the Lord saw her, he had compassion for her and said to her, "Do not weep." Then he came forward and touched the bier, and the bearers stood still. And he said, "Young man, I say to you, rise!" The dead man sat up and began to speak, and Jesus gave him to his mother. Fear seized all of them; and they glorified God, saying, "A great prophet has risen among us!" and "God has looked favorably on his people!" This word about him spread throughout Judea and all the surrounding country.

—Luke 7:11–17

Reflect

Funeral processions rely on custom and tradition, and yet even here Jesus is prepared to act in a new way. He recognizes life in the hope and love of the distressed mother and sympathetic crowd. He shows them that their hopes are not dashed, that love is not over. I look for hope in my own sorrow and grief, knowing that love is never over.

Pray

Help me, Lord, to see how you are at work, bringing life even in seemingly impossible circumstances. Help me to be open about my grief and honest about my fears. Help me recognize your encouragement when it comes.

Is Life Worth the Cost?

Peter began to say to him, "Look, we have left everything and followed you." Jesus said, "Truly I tell you, there is no one who has left house or brothers or sisters or mother or father or children or fields, for my sake and for the sake of the good news, who will not receive a hundredfold now in this age—houses, brothers and sisters, mothers and children, and fields, with persecutions—and in the age to come eternal life. But many who are first will be last, and the last will be first."

—Mark 10:28–31

Reflect

Jesus knew that it was not easy for Peter and the other disciples to let go of the lives they had in order to follow him. He knows that this is not easy for us today either. We can be as blunt as Peter and ask from time to time, "Lord, I feel the pain of giving up something for this life I choose with you. Will it always be pain and sacrifice?"

Pray

Jesus who I follow, I make space in my prayer today for all who have heard the gospel call, for people who have left everything. I try to let go of whatever keeps me from following you wholeheartedly. Encourage my heart and give me hope. May all of us who follow you be signs to one another of purpose and joy.

17

When I'm in a Painful, Frightening Place

Then the assembly rose as a body and brought Jesus before
Pilate. They began to accuse him, saying, "We found this
man perverting our nation, forbidding us to pay taxes to the
emperor, and saying that he himself is the Messiah, a king."
Then Pilate asked him, "Are you the king of the Jews?" He
answered, "You say so." Then Pilate said to the chief priests
and the crowds, "I find no basis for an accusation against this
man." But they were insistent and said, "He stirs up the
people by teaching throughout all Judea, from Galilee where
he began even to this place."

When Pilate heard this, he asked whether the man was a
Galilean. And when he learned that he was under Herod's
jurisdiction, he sent him off to Herod, who was himself in
Jerusalem at that time. When Herod saw Jesus, he was very
glad, for he had been wanting to see him for a long time,
because he had heard about him and was hoping to see him
perform some sign. He questioned him at some length, but
Jesus gave him no answer. The chief priests and the scribes
stood by, vehemently accusing him. Even Herod with his
soldiers treated him with contempt and mocked him; then he
put an elegant robe on him, and sent him back to Pilate. That

same day Herod and Pilate became friends with each other;
before this they had been enemies.

Pilate then called together the chief priests, the leaders, and
the people, and said to them, "You brought me this man as
one who was perverting the people; and here I have examined
him in your presence and have not found this man guilty of
any of your charges against him. Neither has Herod, for he
sent him back to us. Indeed, he has done nothing to deserve
death. I will therefore have him flogged and release him."
Then they all shouted out together, "Away with this fellow!
Release Barabbas for us!" (This was a man who had been put
in prison for an insurrection that had taken place in the city,
and for murder.) Pilate, wanting to release Jesus, addressed
them again; but they kept shouting, "Crucify, crucify him!" A
third time he said to them, "Why, what evil has he done? I
have found in him no ground for the sentence of death; I will
therefore have him flogged and then release him." But they
kept urgently demanding with loud shouts that he should be
crucified; and their voices prevailed. So Pilate gave his verdict
that their demand should be granted. He released the man
they asked for, the one who had been put in prison for
insurrection and murder, and he handed Jesus over as
they wished.

—Luke 23:1–25

Reflect

Jesus had to face betrayal by a disciple, judgment before those hostile toward him, and vulnerability to those with the legal power to kill him or let him go. He chose to enter this long, painful process and follow it to its end, which would be the Crucifixion. He went willingly to a terrible place of suffering because it was his calling to do so. What can I draw from Jesus' actions? Have I had to be vulnerable lately? Have I faced betrayal or judgment? Do I feel that I can emulate Jesus' quiet determination and courage?

Pray

Lord, I will never suffer quite as you did before Pilate and the Sanhedrin, but these days I know what it's like to be betrayed by someone I trusted, to be wrongly judged, and for other people to have power over me. I walk in a frightening place because I think it's the right thing to do. Please hold me close and give me courage.

18

How Can I Share My Resources?

When the crowds found out about it, they followed him; and
he welcomed them, and spoke to them about the kingdom of
God, and healed those who needed to be cured.
The day was drawing to a close, and the twelve came to him
and said, "Send the crowd away, so that they may go into the
surrounding villages and countryside, to lodge and get
provisions; for we are here in a deserted place." But he said to
them, "You give them something to eat." They said, "We have
no more than five loaves and two fish—unless we are to go
and buy food for all these people." For there were about five
thousand men. And he said to his disciples, "Make them sit
down in groups of about fifty each." They did so and made
them all sit down. And taking the five loaves and the two fish,
he looked up to heaven, and blessed and broke them, and
gave them to the disciples to set before the crowd. And all ate
and were filled. What was left over was gathered up, twelve
baskets of broken pieces.

—Luke 9:11–17

Reflect

This miracle reveals the heart of God, who cares about our every need. God also expects us to come to the aid of one another and to share what little we have. When we rely on grace and the gifts of God, we will discover an abundance and have leftovers to spare. Who needs my help now? Who can I help in a concrete way—with either my resources or my encouragement?

Pray

Lord, the hunger of the world screams for my attention. But what can I do? Give me the willingness to go beyond myself, to share my resources toward building a community where people love and care for one another. Help me bring my own hunger to you, and may the eyes of gratitude reveal your abundance to me.

The Solution Is to "Abide"

"I am the true vine, and my Father is the vinegrower. He removes every branch in me that bears no fruit. Every branch that bears fruit he prunes to make it bear more fruit. You have already been cleansed by the word that I have spoken to you. Abide in me as I abide in you. Just as the branch cannot bear fruit by itself unless it abides in the vine, neither can you unless you abide in me. I am the vine, you are the branches. Those who abide in me and I in them bear much fruit, because apart from me you can do nothing. Whoever does not abide in me is thrown away like a branch and withers; such branches are gathered, thrown into the fire, and burned. If you abide in me, and my words abide in you, ask for whatever you wish, and it will be done for you. My Father is glorified by this, that you bear much fruit and become my disciples."

—John 15:1–8

Reflect

Jesus invites me to "abide": to rest, to stay, to remain. Perhaps it is a challenge for me because I'm more comfortable acting and doing. I take some time now to ponder how I need to be connected with the very life of Jesus, to know the beating of his heart, to receive life from him just as a branch receives life from the vine.

Pray

Teach me, Lord Jesus, what it is to live in you and for you to live in me. Help me to be open in my love for you, to be at ease with you, to find my strength in you. Help me stop my hyperactivity and overthinking long enough to sense your life flowing through my own.

God Has Already Shown Me Favor

Then his father Zechariah was filled with the Holy Spirit and
spoke this prophecy:

"Blessed be the Lord God of Israel,
for he has looked favorably on his people and
redeemed them. . . .
And you, child, will be called the prophet of the Most High;
for you will go before the Lord to prepare his ways,
to give knowledge of salvation to his people
by the forgiveness of their sins.
By the tender mercy of our God,
the dawn from on high will break upon us,
to give light to those who sit in darkness and in the
shadow of death,
to guide our feet into the way of peace."
—Luke 1:67–68, 76–79

Reflect

The Benedictus is a prayer of prophecy in the beginning of the Gospel of Luke about the coming of the Savior. This "Most High" that Zechariah mentions comes not in a cloud of glory but as a vulnerable child, with an ordinary family, in a cold stable. That is the kind of God we have—a humble savior who lights up our lives when we sit in darkness, who guides our weary feet to peace.

Pray

The prophecy of Zechariah is prayed by thousands of people every morning. I read it slowly, letting the words reveal their meaning for me. What bubbles up as I read? Help me sift through these thoughts, Lord, and discover what you want me to know today.

21

Is My Heart Troubled?

"Do not let your hearts be troubled. Believe in God, believe also in me. In my Father's house there are many dwelling places. If it were not so, would I have told you that I go to prepare a place for you? And if I go and prepare a place for you, I will come again and will take you to myself, so that where I am, there you may be also. And you know the way to the place where I am going." Thomas said to him, "Lord, we do not know where you are going. How can we know the way?" Jesus said to him, "I am the way, and the truth, and the life. No one comes to the Father except through me."

—John 14:1–6

Reflect

Perhaps I am sometimes like those Jesus was speaking to here: questioning Jesus while thinking that I'm on my own to work things out. Perhaps my heart is troubled, but I worry over the trouble rather than remind myself of Jesus, who urges me to believe in him and trust him.

Pray

Lord, help me listen to your promises, to receive your assurances, to let you remove troubles from my heart. May I bear in mind that you are with me. I am not alone.

22

Remember That God Took the Initiative

"For God so loved the world that he gave his only Son, so that everyone who believes in him may not perish but may have eternal life.

"Indeed, God did not send the Son into the world to condemn the world, but in order that the world might be saved through him. Those who believe in him are not condemned; but those who do not believe are condemned already, because they have not believed in the name of the only Son of God. And this is the judgment, that the light has come into the world, and people loved darkness rather than light because their deeds were evil. For all who do evil hate the light and do not come to the light, so that their deeds may not be exposed. But those who do what is true come to the light, so that it may be clearly seen that their deeds have been done in God."

—John 3:16–21

Reflect

God took the initiative with the human race. This is how God loves the world: he sent Jesus so that we might truly live. Jesus, the Word of God, seeks a home in our hearts and calls us to life—eternal life. He offers light and the option of turning from evil. How do I see God's light at work in my life? How can I take comfort and courage from God's light and love?

Pray

Help me, God of love, to pause in my prayer and recognize what you are already doing. Remind me that I can choose to live in your light. As I consider how you so love the world, I pray for your creation, for all your people. May we all receive Jesus and be brought to life.

23

I Am a Beloved Child of God

As the people were filled with expectation, and all were questioning in their hearts concerning John, whether he might be the Messiah, John answered all of them by saying, "I baptize you with water; but one who is more powerful than I is coming; I am not worthy to untie the thong of his sandals. He will baptize you with the Holy Spirit and fire." . . . Now when all the people were baptized, and when Jesus also had been baptized and was praying, the heaven was opened, and the Holy Spirit descended upon him in bodily form like a dove. And a voice came from heaven, "You are my Son, the Beloved; with you I am well pleased."

—Luke 3:15–16, 21–22

Reflect

God always speaks to Jesus in an intimate and joyful fashion. In essence, he says: "You are my beloved Son; I am pleased with you. I love you deeply. Your whole being springs from me. I am your Father." Jesus answers, "Abba"—"beloved Father." Jesus' whole life reveals trust. He hands himself over unconditionally to his Father. How do I hand myself over to God? How can I work toward surrendering and trusting entirely in the Lord?

Pray

God, I ponder the love you have lavished upon me also, calling me your child. You are the tender and compassionate Mother of my life. You are the faithful Father, the rock on which I stand. Your love is everlasting. Your faithfulness is eternal.

24

Help Me Focus on My Purpose While Suffering

"The Son of Man must undergo great suffering, and be rejected by the elders, chief priests, and scribes, and be killed, and on the third day be raised."

Then he said to them all, "If any want to become my followers, let them deny themselves and take up their cross daily and follow me. For those who want to save their life will lose it, and those who lose their life for my sake will save it. What does it profit them if they gain the whole world, but lose or forfeit themselves?"

—Luke 9:22–25

Reflect

Jesus states clearly that his project to save the world will end in earthly disaster for himself. He does not simply give up and abandon humankind to its malice. He suffers for a reason, and his purpose takes precedence over all else. How does Jesus' sacrifice affect the way I view my own or others' suffering?

Pray

Lord Jesus, you know that I endure some suffering, too. I don't think you're saying that all suffering is good, but you remind me that my purpose—while suffering or at any other time—will transcend whatever I'm going through. I don't want to spend my life only looking after myself and trying to avoid pain and hurt. I want to be free, as you were, to suffer when necessary for the purpose of living out your love, wisdom, patience, and compassion right now, in my circumstances.

25

Weighed Down with Sorrow

But on the first day of the week, at early dawn, they came to
the tomb, taking the spices that they had prepared. They
found the stone rolled away from the tomb, but when they
went in, they did not find the body. While they were
perplexed about this, suddenly two men in dazzling clothes
stood beside them. The women were terrified and bowed
their faces to the ground, but the men said to them, "Why do
you look for the living among the dead? He is not here, but
has risen. Remember how he told you, while he was still in
Galilee, that the Son of Man must be handed over to sinners,
and be crucified, and on the third day rise again." Then they
remembered his words, and returning from the tomb, they
told all this to the eleven and to all the rest. Now it was Mary
Magdalene, Joanna, Mary the mother of James, and the other
women with them who told this to the apostles. But these
words seemed to them an idle tale, and they did not believe
them. But Peter got up and ran to the tomb; stooping and
looking in, he saw the linen cloths by themselves; then he
went home, amazed at what had happened.

—Luke 24:1–12

Reflect

We can picture the women moving through the garden with heavy hearts, oblivious to the dawning spring morning. They are also oblivious to the glorious presence of the risen Christ not a stone's throw away. And yet these women are the first witnesses to the Resurrection. They reveal the qualities of good disciples in their capacity to believe. Do I feel oblivious to the goodness and promise of hope around me? Do I struggle to see help right around the corner?

Pray

Lord, help me realize that when I am weighed down with sorrow, anxiety, or hopelessness, you are no farther from me than you were from the women in that garden. I want to treat this message of the Resurrection not as an idle tale but as good news that transforms our world and gives hope to everyone. Open my eyes to your help and hope, Lord. I need it.

26

God Is Doing the Work

He also said, "The kingdom of God is as if someone would scatter seed on the ground, and would sleep and rise night and day, and the seed would sprout and grow, he does not know how. The earth produces of itself, first the stalk, then the head, then the full grain in the head. But when the grain is ripe, at once he goes in with his sickle, because the harvest has come."

He also said, "With what can we compare the kingdom of God, or what parable will we use for it? It is like a mustard seed, which, when sown upon the ground, is the smallest of all the seeds on earth; yet when it is sown it grows up and becomes the greatest of all shrubs, and puts forth large branches, so that the birds of the air can make nests in its shade."

With many such parables he spoke the word to them, as they were able to hear it; he did not speak to them except in parables, but he explained everything in private to his disciples.

—Mark 4:26–34

Reflect

The reign of God exists in our hopeful activity, patient waiting, and inspired observation. God is the one acting in our world. We only have to recognize that activity, express our gratitude, and participate with it.

Pray

Thank you, Lord, for this most consoling of images. I was not brought into this world to help you out of a mess. You, above all, are the one who is working. Your dynamism, active in nature from the beginning of time, should humble me. You are the force of growth, and if you privilege me with the chance to add incrementally to that growth, that is your gift to me, not mine to you.

27

My Neediness Will Not Drive Jesus Away

A leper came to him begging him, and kneeling he said to him, "If you choose, you can make me clean." Moved with pity, Jesus stretched out his hand and touched him, and said to him, "I do choose. Be made clean!" Immediately the leprosy left him, and he was made clean. After sternly warning him he sent him away at once, saying to him, "See that you say nothing to anyone; but go, show yourself to the priest, and offer for your cleansing what Moses commanded, as a testimony to them." But he went out and began to proclaim it freely, and to spread the word, so that Jesus could no longer go into a town openly, but stayed out in the country; and people came to him from every quarter.

—Mark 1:40–45

Reflect

In this Gospel passage, Jesus is moved with pity. Leprosy was a living death: the sufferer was isolated from family and community and had to cry out, "Unclean, unclean!" when anyone approached. Touching the leper made Jesus ritually unclean also. There are no lengths to which Jesus would not go to help this man. He touched him, spoke to him, and gave him freedom to be fully human again. What isolation or un-wholeness do I bring to the Lord? How will Jesus help me become fully human again?

Pray

I spend a few moments with the leper before his cure and then meet him afterward. What might he say to me about faith in Jesus? About my pity for others in need? Jesus, the leper knew his need and trusted that you could help him. I come to you with the same attitude—not hiding my neediness, not hesitant about bringing it before you—and I listen now for your encouraging response.

28

Light Overcomes Darkness

Again Jesus spoke to them, saying, "I am the light of the world. Whoever follows me will never walk in darkness but will have the light of life." Then the Pharisees said to him, "You are testifying on your own behalf; your testimony is not valid." Jesus answered, "Even if I testify on my own behalf, my testimony is valid because I know where I have come from and where I am going, but you do not know where I come from or where I am going. You judge by human standards; I judge no one. Yet even if I do judge, my judgment is valid; for it is not I alone who judge, but I and the Father who sent me. In your law it is written that the testimony of two witnesses is valid. I testify on my own behalf, and the Father who sent me testifies on my behalf."

Then they said to him, "Where is your Father?" Jesus answered, "You know neither me nor my Father. If you knew me, you would know my Father also." He spoke these words while he was teaching in the treasury of the temple, but no one arrested him, because his hour had not yet come.

—John 8:12–20

Reflect

On the first day of creation, God flooded the heavens and the earth with divine radiance by uttering the mighty words "Let there be light." No matter how dark things may seem, I remind myself that darkness can never overpower light. I turn to Christ, the light of the world.

Pray

I pray with the words of St. Benedict: "O gracious and Holy Father, give us wisdom to perceive you, diligence to seek you, patience to wait for you, eyes to behold you, a heart to meditate upon you, and a life to proclaim you; through the power of the Spirit of Jesus Christ our Lord."

29

Jesus Speaks When We're Ready

"I still have many things to say to you, but you cannot bear
them now. When the Spirit of truth comes, he will guide you
into all the truth; for he will not speak on his own, but will
speak whatever he hears, and he will declare to you the things
that are to come. He will glorify me, because he will take
what is mine and declare it to you. All that the Father has is
mine. For this reason I said that he will take what is mine and
declare it to you."

—John 16:12–15

Reflect

Jesus still speaks to us. He tells us that prayer helps us grow in love, in friendship, in understanding the ways of God. The Spirit assists us, mediating God's message, helping us recognize how our way of living conforms to what God asks of us and how it does not. Am I ready to hear Jesus' message to me? Am I ready to look at which parts of my life conform to God's desires for me and which parts do not?

Pray

"You cannot bear them now," you said. Lord, you time your interventions for my readiness. The prophet Isaiah said that those who wait upon you shall renew their strength. May I learn how to wait upon you. Strengthen my ability to receive and listen to your Spirit, to remember that your Spirit speaks your word to me.

30

All Sinners Have a Future

One of the Pharisees asked Jesus to eat with him, and he went into the Pharisee's house and took his place at the table. And a woman in the city, who was a sinner, having learned that he was eating in the Pharisee's house, brought an alabaster jar of ointment. She stood behind him at his feet, weeping, and began to bathe his feet with her tears and to dry them with her hair. Then she continued kissing his feet and anointing them with the ointment. Now when the Pharisee who had invited him saw it, he said to himself, "If this man were a prophet, he would have known who and what kind of woman this is who is touching him—that she is a sinner." Jesus spoke up and said to him, "Simon, I have something to say to you."

"Teacher," he replied, "speak." "A certain creditor had two debtors; one owed five hundred denarii, and the other fifty. When they could not pay, he canceled the debts for both of them. Now which of them will love him more?" Simon answered, "I suppose the one for whom he canceled the greater debt." And Jesus said to him, "You have judged rightly." Then turning toward the woman, he said to Simon, "Do you see this woman? I entered your house; you gave me no water for my feet, but she has bathed my feet with her tears and dried them with her hair. You gave me no kiss, but from the time I came in she has not stopped kissing my feet.

You did not anoint my head with oil, but she has anointed
my feet with ointment. Therefore, I tell you, her sins, which
were many, have been forgiven; hence she has shown great
love. But the one to whom little is forgiven, loves little." Then
he said to her, "Your sins are forgiven." But those who were at
the table with him began to say among themselves, "Who is
this who even forgives sins?" And he said to the woman,
"Your faith has saved you; go in peace."
—Luke 7:36–50

Reflect

Simon had life mapped out: he had decided who deserved his attention and how they might be honored. He invited Jesus as a guest but withheld courtesy—he was prepared to listen to the words of Jesus but not ready to receive them in his heart. The Pharisee is surprised, shocked even, when Jesus allows a sinner to touch him. He has yet to understand that Jesus welcomes and heals sinners. But he does not think of *himself* as in need of healing. Did he perhaps reflect later over this incident and learn something? What about me? Do I think I'm in need of healing?

Pray

I ask God to help me, as I review my life, to recognize and remove any ways in which I resist God's Word. All sinners have a future, Lord. Let me never despair of myself, since you do not do so. Forgiveness is for all, and the greater the need, the more generous is God's response.

31

Help Me Receive Your Peace

Then they told what had happened on the road, and how he had been made known to them in the breaking of the bread. While they were talking about this, Jesus himself stood among them and said to them, "Peace be with you." They were startled and terrified, and thought that they were seeing a ghost. He said to them, "Why are you frightened, and why do doubts arise in your hearts? Look at my hands and my feet; see that it is I myself. Touch me and see; for a ghost does not have flesh and bones as you see that I have." And when he had said this, he showed them his hands and his feet. While in their joy they were disbelieving and still wondering, he said to them, "Have you anything here to eat?" They gave him a piece of broiled fish, and he took it and ate in their presence. Then he said to them, "These are my words that I spoke to you while I was still with you—that everything written about me in the law of Moses, the prophets, and the psalms must be fulfilled." Then he opened their minds to understand the scriptures, and he said to them, "Thus it is written, that the Messiah is to suffer and to rise from the dead on the third day, and that repentance and forgiveness of sins is to be proclaimed in his name to all nations, beginning from Jerusalem. You are witnesses of these things."

—Luke 24:35–48

Reflect

Jesus' greeting is "peace." It's like the signature tune of a radio show; we know that, with the greeting of peace, Jesus is near. Can I allow that word to flow through the silence and the words of my prayer today?

Pray

The disciples received reports of Jesus' Resurrection and were talking about it, yet they were not ready to receive this message from Jesus himself: "Peace be with you." Jesus, help me receive this sacred story about your resurrection. Help me also be willing, this day, to believe and accept your gift of peace.

32

Regain a Sense of Wonder and Joy

People were bringing little children to him in order that he might touch them; and the disciples spoke sternly to them. But when Jesus saw this, he was indignant and said to them, "Let the little children come to me; do not stop them; for it is to such as these that the kingdom of God belongs. Truly I tell you, whoever does not receive the kingdom of God as a little child will never enter it." And he took them up in his arms, laid his hands on them, and blessed them.

—Mark 10:13–16

Reflect

The disciples were protective of Jesus, believing that they should decide who was worthy of his attention. In this time of prayer, I let all my concerns come before God, being careful not to let through only the ones that I think are presentable.

Pray

Lord, I forget to nourish my childlike qualities. Do I come to you openly, expecting love? Do I allow myself to wonder and ask questions? Am I too self-conscious to be joyful and willing to play? Thank you for your always-open arms. Help me go to them every day.

33

Jesus Calls Me as I Am

As he walked by the Sea of Galilee, he saw two brothers,
Simon, who is called Peter, and Andrew his brother, casting a
net into the lake—for they were fishermen. And he said to
them, "Follow me, and I will make you fish for people."
Immediately they left their nets and followed him. As he went
from there, he saw two other brothers, James son of Zebedee
and his brother John, in the boat with their father Zebedee,
mending their nets, and he called them. Immediately they left
the boat and their father, and followed him.

—Matthew 4:18–22

Reflect

Jesus called the fishermen, speaking to them in terms they recognized. Jesus calls me as I am, wanting me to use my skills and abilities to draw others to life. In the middle of any ordinary day, Jesus walks by, sees me, singles me out from the crowd, speaks to me, and invites me to be a disciple. What attracts me to Jesus? What helps me respond generously to him? Am I a close follower of his, or do I keep my eye on him only occasionally?

Pray

Lord, those first disciples—Peter, Andrew, James, and John—didn't change anything about themselves before they responded to you; in fact, the story tells us that they followed you immediately. I hold back from following you sometimes because I keep feeling that I need to be a better person, or more knowledgeable about the faith, or more talented. Help me see what might be holding me back today. Help me respond in confidence simply because you have called my name.

34

Can I Call Out for Help?

As Jesus went on from there, two blind men followed him, crying loudly, "Have mercy on us, Son of David!" When he entered the house, the blind men came to him; and Jesus said to them, "Do you believe that I am able to do this?" They said to him, "Yes, Lord." Then he touched their eyes and said, "According to your faith let it be done to you." And their eyes were opened. Then Jesus sternly ordered them, "See that no one knows of this." But they went away and spread the news about him throughout that district.

—Matthew 9:27–31

Reflect

How could these men follow Jesus if they could not see? By hearing his voice, perhaps. Or maybe others led them to him. How did they know what to ask for? They knew they needed physical and spiritual sight, so they asked for more than sight: they asked for mercy. Their faith in Jesus opened their hearts to appeal to him. Their faith connected with Jesus' power, and they were healed. They knew their need for God and for others; they did not hide their need and thus were healed. Am I willing to call out for the healing I need?

Pray

Jesus the healer, I can let so many things get in the way of a simple request for your help. Whether it's the opinions of others or my own sense of guilt or inferiority, the effect is the same: I linger in pain and hunger for a better life. Help me ask for what I need today.

35

Am I Lost?

[Jesus said,] "What do you think? If a shepherd has a hundred sheep, and one of them has gone astray, does he not leave the ninety-nine on the mountains and go in search of the one that went astray? And if he finds it, truly I tell you, he rejoices over it more than over the ninety-nine that never went astray. So it is not the will of your Father in heaven that one of these little ones should be lost."

—Matthew 18:12–14

Reflect

Every Gospel passage tells us something about God. Here I learn that God has a particular tenderness and care for everyone, especially for those who have gone astray. This is a comfort to me because I often lose my way in life. I know that God is watching out for me always. Can I trust today that God is more interested in my struggles and failures than in the "successes" of so many other people who seem to be doing well?

Pray

Good Shepherd, I feel so lost and unwanted right now. Is anyone really looking out for me? Does anyone even miss me? If you really are searching for me, God, please find me soon.

36

Doubting with the Best of Them

When John heard in prison what the Messiah was doing, he sent word by his disciples and said to him, "Are you the one who is to come, or are we to wait for another?" Jesus answered them, "Go and tell John what you hear and see: the blind receive their sight, the lame walk, the lepers are cleansed, the deaf hear, the dead are raised, and the poor have good news brought to them. And blessed is anyone who takes no offence at me."

As they went away, Jesus began to speak to the crowds about John: "What did you go out into the wilderness to look at? A reed shaken by the wind? What then did you go out to see? Someone dressed in soft robes? Look, those who wear soft robes are in royal palaces. What then did you go out to see? A prophet? Yes, I tell you, and more than a prophet. This is the one about whom it is written,

'See, I am sending my messenger ahead of you,
who will prepare your way before you.'
Truly I tell you, among those born of women no one has arisen greater than John the Baptist; yet the least in the kingdom of heaven is greater than he."

— Matthew 11:2–11

Reflect

There is real comfort in this story. John the Baptist, the powerful, austere man who held such sway among the Jews, still had his moments of darkness. Imprisoned in Herod's dungeon, he wondered: *Am I a fool? Is this all there is? Was I wrong about Jesus?* "Go and tell John what you hear and see . . . the blind receive their sight . . ."! What do I see and hear? Do I see the signs of God's kingdom breaking through in the world around me? What do they look like? If I don't see any positive signs, why not? Do I need to look again, or look differently? Am I somehow looking for "soft robes and royal palaces" when God is offering me a prophet?

Pray

Lord, it's sort of a relief to know that even a believer like John the Baptist had his doubts about you. Even he grew discouraged and wondered if he'd gotten it all wrong. That means that my doubts and discouragement and confusion don't set me apart as an especially faulty spiritual person. Thank you for the signs of your presence that are already in my life. I don't see many of them now—please open my eyes and my heart to this grace-filled reality.

37

A Less-Than-Perfect Family History

An account of the genealogy of Jesus the Messiah, the son of
David, the son of Abraham.
Abraham was the father of Isaac, and Isaac the father of Jacob,
and Jacob the father of Judah and his brothers, and Judah the
father of Perez and Zerah by Tamar, and Perez the father of
Hezron, and Hezron the father of Aram, and Aram the father
of Aminadab, and Aminadab the father of Nahshon, and
Nahshon the father of Salmon, and Salmon the father of Boaz
by Rahab, and Boaz the father of Obed by Ruth, and Obed
the father of Jesse, and Jesse the father of King David.
And David was the father of Solomon by the wife of Uriah,
and Solomon the father of Rehoboam, and Rehoboam the
father of Abijah, and Abijah the father of Asaph, and Asaph
the father of Jehoshaphat, and Jehoshaphat the father of
Joram, and Joram the father of Uzziah, and Uzziah the father
of Jotham, and Jotham the father of Ahaz, and Ahaz the
father of Hezekiah, and Hezekiah the father of Manasseh, and
Manasseh the father of Amos, and Amos the father of Josiah,
and Josiah the father of Jechoniah and his brothers, at the
time of the deportation to Babylon.
And after the deportation to Babylon: Jechoniah was the
father of Salathiel, and Salathiel the father of Zerubbabel, and
Zerubbabel the father of Abiud, and Abiud the father of

Eliakim, and Eliakim the father of Azor, and Azor the father
of Zadok, and Zadok the father of Achim, and Achim the
father of Eliud, and Eliud the father of Eleazar, and Eleazar
the father of Matthan, and Matthan the father of Jacob, and
Jacob the father of Joseph the husband of Mary, of whom
Jesus was born, who is called the Messiah.
So all the generations from Abraham to David are fourteen
generations; and from David to the deportation to Babylon,
fourteen generations; and from the deportation to Babylon to
the Messiah, fourteen generations.

—Matthew 1:1–17

Reflect

In the Jewish tradition, a person's genealogy was quite important, which is why this one of Jesus' was included in the Gospel. This passage looks unsparingly at Jesus' ancestry. Matthew points out that Jesus' forebears included children born of incest (Perez), of mixed races (Boaz), and of adultery (Solomon). Family tradition and social expectations play their part in any person's life, but deep down we need to know what God is inviting us to be. We are God's beloveds, and a high destiny awaits us. We are to reveal to the world something of God's own self. What aspect of my own family history or expectations do I feel the need to overcome? What is God's special call for me?

Pray

God, you entered our human history with all the episodes that proud people would be ashamed of. Teach me to accept my humanity, my genes, and my relatives, as you did. Remind me that genetics and family history are only part of my story and that you are writing your sacred story in my life every day. I want to truly live as if your dream for me can transcend any wounds and shadows from my origins.

38

Difficult Decisions and the Need for God's Prompting

Now the birth of Jesus the Messiah took place in this way.
When his mother Mary had been engaged to Joseph, but
before they lived together, she was found to be with child
from the Holy Spirit. Her husband Joseph, being a righteous
man and unwilling to expose her to public disgrace, planned
to dismiss her quietly. But just when he had resolved to do
this, an angel of the Lord appeared to him in a dream and
said, "Joseph, son of David, do not be afraid to take Mary as
your wife, for the child conceived in her is from the Holy
Spirit. She will bear a son, and you are to name him Jesus, for
he will save his people from their sins." All this took place to
fulfill what had been spoken by the Lord
through the prophet:

"Look, the virgin shall conceive and bear a son,
and they shall name him Emmanuel,"
which means, "God is with us." When Joseph awoke from
sleep, he did as the angel of the Lord commanded him; he
took her as his wife.

—Matthew 1:18–24

Reflect

Joseph faced a heartbreaking dilemma. His life was in turmoil because he loved Mary so much. How welcome the angel's message must have been to him, then! How quickly he acted, allowing himself to follow his heart and not allowing his sense of legal obligation to rule. Do I invite the Spirit to prompt me? How ready am I to hear what the Spirit might suggest?

Pray

God of my interior life, in so many sacred stories, your prompting comes from deep within—from dreams and visions, even from sorrow and heartbreak. I'm facing a difficult decision now. Help me discern the right way and act on it. Help me move forward because you give me understanding.

39

When Plans Change and Life Looks Bleak

Now after they had left, an angel of the Lord appeared to
Joseph in a dream and said, "Get up, take the child and his
mother, and flee to Egypt, and remain there until I tell you;
for Herod is about to search for the child, to destroy him."
Then Joseph got up, took the child and his mother by night,
and went to Egypt, and remained there until the death of
Herod. This was to fulfil what had been spoken by the Lord
through the prophet, "Out of Egypt I have called my son."
When Herod saw that he had been tricked by the wise men,
he was infuriated, and he sent and killed all the children in
and around Bethlehem who were two years old or under,
according to the time that he had learned from the wise men.
Then was fulfilled what had been spoken through the
prophet Jeremiah:

"A voice was heard in Ramah,
wailing and loud lamentation,
Rachel weeping for her children;
she refused to be consoled, because they are no more."
—Matthew 2:13–18

Reflect

This is a painful story to read, especially when we think of how this scenario happens over and over again today. Joseph and his tiny family have to become refugees and go by night to a foreign land. Worse, they are unwilling players in a larger scene: Herod's massacre of children. So often, refugees flee from situations of severe violence. And even when we are not refugees, a sudden turn of events can make life seem quite unsafe and our future precarious. What has upset my life's trajectory lately? A death? A job loss? Financial disaster?

Pray

Lord, it helps to understand that, as a Jew in Roman-occupied Palestine, you and your family experienced real insecurity. My situation is not the same as yours, but it feels unsafe and scary. I didn't plan on this! What do I do? Show me the way. And remind me to pray for refugees all over this globe who suffer uncertainty and sometimes great discomfort.

40

Even Jesus Needed a Push

On the third day there was a wedding in Cana of Galilee, and the mother of Jesus was there. Jesus and his disciples had also been invited to the wedding. When the wine gave out, the mother of Jesus said to him, "They have no wine." And Jesus said to her, "Woman, what concern is that to you and to me? My hour has not yet come." His mother said to the servants, "Do whatever he tells you." Now standing there were six stone water jars for the Jewish rites of purification, each holding twenty or thirty gallons. Jesus said to them, "Fill the jars with water." And they filled them up to the brim. He said to them, "Now draw some out, and take it to the chief steward." So they took it. When the steward tasted the water that had become wine, and did not know where it came from (though the servants who had drawn the water knew), the steward called the bridegroom and said to him, "Everyone serves the good wine first, and then the inferior wine after the guests have become drunk. But you have kept the good wine until now." Jesus did this, the first of his signs, in Cana of Galilee, and revealed his glory; and his disciples believed in him.

—John 2:1–11

Reflect

It appears that Jesus needed a push from someone who loved and knew him and knew his purpose in the world. God sent Jesus into this human life, yet Jesus had to embrace his life mission day by day. When was the last time I purposefully embraced a task or goal because I recognized that it was God's will for me and part of my life calling?

Pray

God, sometimes I see what I need to do, but it can be hard to do it. I'm unsure of myself, or I wonder whether the time is really right. Or maybe I fear the responsibility and the change that might accompany my taking the next step. Go ahead and give me a little push if that's what I need.

41

When Labels Threaten to Limit Me

The next day Jesus decided to go to Galilee. He found Philip
and said to him, "Follow me." Now Philip was from
Bethsaida, the city of Andrew and Peter. Philip found
Nathanael and said to him, "We have found him about
whom Moses in the law and also the prophets wrote, Jesus
son of Joseph from Nazareth." Nathanael said to him, "Can
anything good come out of Nazareth?" Philip said to him,
"Come and see." When Jesus saw Nathanael coming toward
him, he said of him, "Here is truly an Israelite in whom there
is no deceit!" Nathanael asked him, "Where did you get to
know me?" Jesus answered, "I saw you under the fig tree
before Philip called you." Nathanael replied, "Rabbi, you are
the Son of God! You are the King of Israel!" Jesus answered,
"Do you believe because I told you that I saw you under the
fig tree? You will see greater things than these." And he said to
him, "Very truly, I tell you, you will see heaven opened and
the angels of God ascending and descending upon
the Son of Man."
—John 1:43–51

Reflect

"Can anything good come out of Nazareth?" Or, as Nathanael might have been thinking, can anything good come out of that broken home? Can anything good come out of that life that has taken so many wrong turns? Can anything good come out of a person who grew up with violence and addiction? Nathanael's thinking was probably an expression of the culture he grew up in. Most of us know what it's like to be labeled because we come from a certain region or because the small community around us knows our family history and our personal failings. What label am I struggling with as I try to live out God's call in my life?

Pray

I sit with you, Jesus, and think about the labels you had to shatter as you moved ahead in your own life. You patiently listened to God's voice and then bravely did what you were called to do. Help me do the same as I face labels and potential limitations.

42

Give Up the Burden of Vengeance

"You have heard that it was said, 'An eye for an eye and a tooth for a tooth.' But I say to you, Do not resist an evildoer. But if anyone strikes you on the right cheek, turn the other also; and if anyone wants to sue you and take your coat, give your cloak as well; and if anyone forces you to go one mile, go also the second mile. Give to everyone who begs from you, and do not refuse anyone who wants to borrow from you."

—Matthew 5:38–42

Reflect

The principle of an eye for an eye and a tooth for a tooth served to prevent excessive retaliation for an offense. But Jesus wants no retaliation at all. Instead he looks for a generosity of spirit that forgives the offender and returns good for evil. In other words, the burden of vengeance is not on you or me. We don't have to be the judge or jury. What does it feel like to let this truth sink in?

Pray

God, you are just and merciful. You have relieved me of the burden that comes with constant judging of others and myself. I want to live more consistently by Jesus' ethic of generosity toward others. Show me when I begin to feel vengeful rather than gracious. I want to give the huge responsibility of proper judgment to you.

43

God Shows Up in People Who Might Surprise You

John said to [Jesus], "Teacher, we saw someone casting out demons in your name, and we tried to stop him, because he was not following us." But Jesus said, "Do not stop him; for no one who does a deed of power in my name will be able soon afterward to speak evil of me. Whoever is not against us is for us."

—Mark 9:38–40

Reflect

Gathering together and belonging are important human needs, but Jesus shows us how these impulses can lead us astray. The reign of God is advanced wherever good is done, wherever truth is spoken, whenever love wins out. These things can free us to see God's presence in more places than we might expect. Do I tend to look for God's action only in certain people and situations? Have I been missing grace because my mind-set is too insular?

Pray

Lord, help me not to be narrow minded or judgmental but to remain open to your light and life wherever they occur. Maybe I need to get outside my usual sacred spaces. Is there someone I have dismissed who may be just the person I need right now? Have I kept you away by being suspicious of others?

44

Jesus, Set Me Free

Now [Jesus] was teaching in one of the synagogues on the sabbath. And just then there appeared a woman with a spirit that had crippled her for eighteen years. She was bent over and was quite unable to stand up straight. When Jesus saw her, he called her over and said, "Woman, you are set free from your ailment." When he laid his hands on her, immediately she stood up straight and began praising God. But the leader of the synagogue, indignant because Jesus had cured on the sabbath, kept saying to the crowd, "There are six days on which work ought to be done; come on those days and be cured, and not on the sabbath day." But the Lord answered him and said, "You hypocrites! Does not each of you on the sabbath untie his ox or his donkey from the manger, and lead it away to give it water? And ought not this woman, a daughter of Abraham whom Satan bound for eighteen long years, be set free from this bondage on the sabbath day?" When he said this, all his opponents were put to shame; and the entire crowd was rejoicing at all the wonderful things that he was doing.

—Luke 13:10–17

Reflect

Think of the perspective of this woman, unable to stand straight: never able to look anyone in the eye, unable to take her place among any ordinary crowd. She was likely to have been looked down on or overlooked, denied her dignity as a person. Jesus wants to free me of any improper impediments or restrictions. He does not ask me what I can bear, what I am used to, or what I can settle for. He wants to restore me to my proper stature and to let me see as he sees.

Pray

Lord, the people who loved systems more than people were not concerned for this woman to be healed. But you revealed God's true priorities. You freed this woman. And you can free me, too. Is my life misshapen by crippling attachments and misplaced desires? Help me believe that it is your high priority to free me.

45

Jesus Encouraged Mary—and Martha, Too

Now as they went on their way, [Jesus] entered a certain village, where a woman named Martha welcomed him into her home. She had a sister named Mary, who sat at the Lord's feet and listened to what he was saying. But Martha was distracted by her many tasks; so she came to him and asked, "Lord, do you not care that my sister has left me to do all the work by myself? Tell her then to help me." But the Lord answered her, "Martha, Martha, you are worried and distracted by many things; there is need of only one thing. Mary has chosen the better part, which will not be taken away from her."

—Luke 10:38–42

Reflect

Martha took initiative to show hospitality to Jesus. Clearly they were friends because she was free to speak to him bluntly. For Mary, Jesus offered complete welcome to learn as one of the disciples. For Martha, he offered a gentle rebuke because he knew that she—so busy with ministering to those in her home—needed to sit and gain strength and wisdom, too. Can I, like Mary, ignore other demands and simply be with Jesus? Can I, like Martha, speak to Jesus as a friend—and then listen to his response?

Pray

Jesus, I'm grateful that you loved both these women and that you responded to each as she needed. What word do you have for me today? Am I distracted? Working too hard without stopping for spiritual replenishment? Young in the faith and needing to spend a lot of time with your teaching? I want to receive your words as I would receive the words of a dear and trusted friend.

46

What Do I Want Jesus to Do for Me?

As [Jesus] approached Jericho, a blind man was sitting by the roadside begging. When he heard a crowd going by, he asked what was happening. They told him, "Jesus of Nazareth is passing by." Then he shouted, "Jesus, Son of David, have mercy on me!" Those who were in front sternly ordered him to be quiet; but he shouted even more loudly, "Son of David, have mercy on me!" Jesus stood still and ordered the man to be brought to him; and when he came near, he asked him, "What do you want me to do for you?" He said, "Lord, let me see again." Jesus said to him, "Receive your sight; your faith has saved you." Immediately he regained his sight and followed him, glorifying God; and all the people, when they saw it, praised God.

—Luke 18:35–43

Reflect

Jesus does not cure unbidden. He waits to be asked. What may seem from the outside a desperate need could for the sightless be such a habitual state that they could not imagine themselves otherwise. So Jesus asks: What do you want me to do for you? The blind, the starving, and the troubled know what they need and want. Some of the better-off seem to live without desires, not keen to change themselves, complacent. How would I respond if the Lord asked me, "What do you want me to do for you?"

Pray

Jesus, my healer, do I know what I really want you to do for me? Have I settled for a wound that hampers me, yet have grown used to it? Do I find comfort in others' attention to me because of this wound or problem—and would I rather have the attention than get better? Help me sort this out. I want to be honest with you, Lord, and I really do want the healing I need.

47

The Intensity of Jesus' Love for Me

[Jesus said to his disciples,] "As the Father has loved me, so
I have loved you; abide in my love. If you keep my
commandments, you will abide in my love, just as I have kept
my Father's commandments and abide in his love. I have said
these things to you so that my joy may be in you, and that
your joy may be complete.

"This is my commandment, that you love one another as
I have loved you. No one has greater love than this, to lay
down one's life for one's friends. You are my friends if you do
what I command you."

—John 15:9–14

Reflect

Before we can love one another as Jesus has loved us, we need to allow ourselves to experience Jesus' love. Jesus says very clearly that his love for us is of the same quality and intensity of God's love for him—and God called Jesus his beloved Son. Do I dare think of myself as God's beloved daughter or son?

Pray

Jesus, you know that every love I have known in this world has been flawed. You also know how much I have felt—or haven't felt—that I was a beloved child of my mother or father. Can you break through my inability to believe that you love me so much? Will you help me at least begin to sense the great intensity with which you love me?

48

Jesus Calls Me Friend

"I do not call you servants any longer, because the servant does not know what the master is doing; but I have called you friends, because I have made known to you everything that I have heard from my Father. You did not choose me but I chose you. And I appointed you to go and bear fruit, fruit that will last, so that the Father will give you whatever you ask him in my name. I am giving you these commands so that you may love one another."

—John 15:15–17

Reflect

It's profound to think of myself as a friend of Jesus, one to whom he reveals spiritual truth. A friend listens to me, stays with me when life is hard and when I'm not doing well. Jesus' friendship—my connection to him—will make it possible for my life to be fruitful, even though I am not perfect and have many lessons to learn. What kind of fruit am I called to bear?

Pray

Jesus, your choosing me gives me a sense of my place in the world, a sense of purpose. You are not waiting until I became a better person; you choose me here and now. What do you want me to do with my life today?

49

Jesus Does Not Sugarcoat Pain

[Jesus said to his disciples,] "Very truly, I tell you, you will weep and mourn, but the world will rejoice; you will have pain, but your pain will turn into joy. When a woman is in labor, she has pain, because her hour has come. But when her child is born, she no longer remembers the anguish because of the joy of having brought a human being into the world. So you have pain now; but I will see you again, and your hearts will rejoice, and no one will take your joy from you. On that day you will ask nothing of me. Very truly, I tell you, if you ask anything of the Father in my name, he will give it to you."

—John 16:20–23

Reflect

Most leaders tell their followers only about the benefits of their cause. Jesus is brutally honest with us about the pain we will experience. While the world goes on its merry way, we will experience much pain: the pain of seeing people reject God's help, the pain caused by a world that seems to run on hatred and bigotry, the pain of being misunderstood even by people close to us because we choose God's kingdom over everything else. Jesus did not say he would rescue us from this pain. He did point out, though, that pain in the life of faith turns into joy. Do I think of pain as something that I must avoid at all costs? When I'm in pain, do I feel that it's because I'm spiritually weak or somehow "outside" of God's will?

Pray

Lord, thank you for not sugarcoating what it means to live with spiritual integrity. Sometimes I think that pain is just another sign of personal failure, but your words remind me that at times pain is actually proof that I'm doing exactly the best thing. Help me endure this pain until you have transformed it into joy.

50

We're Meant to Need Our Friends

One day, while [Jesus] was teaching, Pharisees and teachers of
the law were sitting nearby (they had come from every village
of Galilee and Judea and from Jerusalem); and the power of
the Lord was with him to heal. Just then some men came,
carrying a paralyzed man on a bed. They were trying to bring
him in and lay him before Jesus; but finding no way to bring
him in because of the crowd, they went up on the roof and let
him down with his bed through the tiles into the middle of
the crowd in front of Jesus. When he saw their faith, he said,
"Friend, your sins are forgiven you."

—Luke 5:17–20

Reflect

Without the help of his determined friends, the paralytic could never have made his way to Jesus to be healed. We don't even know if the paralytic asked to be taken to Jesus—did he even have faith that Jesus could help him? It doesn't appear that Jesus asked for clarification, only that he attended to the man who needed his help. Do I push away those who would help me? Do I think that everything depends on my personal faith?

Pray

Lord, is it possible that my own sense of pride and self-sufficiency get in the way of your helping me sometimes? This story shows me that it's okay to be helped by our friends. Maybe that's how it's meant to work—in community, not each person for him- or herself. I need to adjust my way of seeing this. Help me do that. Open my heart not only to help others but also to receive help.

51

Forgiveness Involves Mind, Body, and Soul

Then the scribes and Pharisees began to question, "Who is this who speaks blasphemies? Who can forgive sins but God alone?" When Jesus perceived their questionings, he answered them, "Why do you raise such questions in your hearts? Which is easier, to say, 'Your sins are forgiven,' or to say, 'Stand up and walk'? But so that you may know that the Son of Man has authority on earth to forgive sins"—he said to the one who was paralyzed—"I say to you, stand up and take your bed and go to your home." Immediately he stood up before them, took what he had been lying on, and went to his home, glorifying God. Amazement seized all of them, and they glorified God and were filled with awe, saying, "We have seen strange things today."

—Luke 5:21–26

Reflect

Jesus' point is powerful: if he can heal our bodies, then certainly he has the power to forgive our sins. In fact, the two may go together more than we think. Jesus understood, those many centuries ago, that a person is not simply a spirit inside a body. Instead, the spiritual, mental, physical, and emotional are intertwined; the person is a whole, and one part affects the rest. Do I go through the day as if my physical and spiritual existence were two different entities? Can I allow Jesus' interaction with my whole self?

Pray

Jesus, you are the great healer. But you don't stop at that: you want the whole person to be free and healthy. May I apprehend your work in every part of my life. May I welcome your healing in my body, my emotions, my memories, my thoughts, my everything.

52

The Reality about Suffering

Then he looked up at his disciples and said:
"Blessed are you who are poor,
for yours is the kingdom of God.
"Blessed are you who are hungry now,
for you will be filled.
"Blessed are you who weep now,
for you will laugh.
"Blessed are you when people hate you, and when they
exclude you, revile you, and defame you on account of the
Son of Man. Rejoice in that day and leap for joy, for surely
your reward is great in heaven; for that is what their ancestors
did to the prophets.
"But woe to you who are rich,
for you have received your consolation.
"Woe to you who are full now,
for you will be hungry.
"Woe to you who are laughing now,
for you will mourn and weep.
"Woe to you when all speak well of you, for that is what their
ancestors did to the false prophets."
—Luke 6:20–26

Reflect

There are no glossy images here! Who wants to be poorer, sadder, involved in conflict, excluded, or demeaned? Jesus does not ask us to seek out discomfort, but he wants us to realize that God always holds a brighter promise for us. Jesus announces that God's kingdom looks different from what the world calls happiness or success. There's a reality that overshadows all other perceptions. Can I begin to see the way Jesus describes life in these verses? Do I dare believe that my suffering is but a shadow in a life of joy and blessedness?

Pray

Lord, you ask me to believe something that's pretty fantastic: that I am blessed when I mourn, when I'm hungry, when I'm hated. You also ask me to see others as blessed when they suffer. Please transform my vision of this world. I want to see the reality you are describing. I want to be free even as I suffer some of these trials you name.

53

I Need Peace That's Real

[Jesus said to his disciples,] "Peace I leave with you; my peace I give to you. I do not give to you as the world gives. Do not let your hearts be troubled, and do not let them be afraid."

—John 14:27

Reflect

Jesus' farewell wish is "Peace!" His gift of peace is not a state of being but a relationship. It is the fruit of our deeply abiding in him. This relationship of peace will never fail. It enabled the disciples to endure suffering and rejection. The peace that Jesus gives is available to me, too; I do not have to do anything to receive it. But maybe that's the problem—I want to do something to earn what Jesus offers as a free gift.

Pray

Lord, help me do nothing in this time of prayer but be ready to receive what you offer. As I emerge from prayer each day, may I be more filled with peace than when I began. And may my prayer shape me to be an instrument of your peace in a divided world.

54

We Don't Have to Understand It All Now

"You heard me say to you, 'I am going away, and I am coming to you.' If you loved me, you would rejoice that I am going to the Father, because the Father is greater than I. And now I have told you this before it occurs, so that when it does occur, you may believe. I will no longer talk much with you, for the ruler of this world is coming. He has no power over me; but I do as the Father has commanded me, so that the world may know that I love the Father."

—John 14:28–31

Reflect

Jesus knows that his disciples do not understand the events as they unfold. They don't understand why it's a good thing that he will go away. They don't understand that even though the "ruler of the world" is coming, God's purpose still goes forward. Jesus knows that his closest followers do not understand so much of what is happening, yet he continues on his way and gives them reassurance. I can imagine how they felt: confused, dismayed, afraid. Does my need to understand sometimes get in the way of my believing what Jesus says?

Pray

Jesus, I do want to walk in faith. That's hard to do when I don't know what's going to happen next. It's hard to have faith when I have this hunger to explain everything, when I'm moved by this drive to solve every problem. Give me the patience and the grace and the faith to walk with you when I don't yet understand what is happening and why.

55

Spiritual Progress Does Not Require Genius

Jesus rejoiced in the Holy Spirit and said, "I thank you, Father, Lord of heaven and earth, because you have hidden these things from the wise and the intelligent and have revealed them to infants; yes, Father, for such was your gracious will. All things have been handed over to me by my Father; and no one knows who the Son is except the Father, or who the Father is except the Son and anyone to whom the Son chooses to reveal him."

Then turning to the disciples, Jesus said to them privately, "Blessed are the eyes that see what you see! For I tell you that many prophets and kings desired to see what you see, but did not see it, and to hear what you hear, but did not hear it."

—Luke 10:21–24

Reflect

A person can be simple, unlearned, in the dark, and lost—and yet God can reveal to that person all that is necessary to know life. For me to rejoice in the Holy Spirit is to be aware of the Father's infinite and unconditional love poured out on me. Are there moments in my life when I have felt such love? Is there something preventing me from experiencing such love today?

Pray

I thank you, Father, because you have revealed your love to me. You didn't wait for me to grow wise. You didn't require that I work it all out philosophically. You invited me to you, and I respond as I choose. May I always respond by meeting you, listening to you, receiving your love, and sharing it with others.

56

Prayer Changes Me, Not God

Then Jesus told them a parable about their need to pray always and not to lose heart. He said, "In a certain city there was a judge who neither feared God nor had respect for people. In that city there was a widow who kept coming to him and saying, 'Grant me justice against my opponent.' For a while he refused; but later he said to himself, 'Though I have no fear of God and no respect for anyone, yet because this widow keeps bothering me, I will grant her justice, so that she may not wear me out by continually coming.'" And the Lord said, "Listen to what the unjust judge says. And will not God grant justice to his chosen ones who cry to him day and night? Will he delay long in helping them? I tell you, he will quickly grant justice to them. And yet, when the Son of Man comes, will he find faith on earth?"

—Luke 18:1–8

Reflect

Our persistence in prayer does not change God's mind. Instead it prepares our own heart by strengthening our desire for God. Jesus wishes us to pray always and not lose heart. Am I persistent, or do I give up after time has gone by? Do I believe God will hear and answer?

Pray

Lord, I hear you telling me to persist in prayer, to entreat God as long as I need to. You say he will quickly grant justice. But then I think of good people suffering famine, AIDS, loss of children, sickness, and death, even though they pray to God. I think of the Jews in Auschwitz, still singing the psalms as they walked into the gas chambers. Surely there are times when you delay in helping us? At times like this I turn to the memory of your Passion and your agonized prayer in the garden. You have faced a dark and apparently empty heaven yet stayed faithful. Keep me with you. Help me to be constant, Lord. Renew my failing confidence when your answer is, "Wait . . . wait . . . wait a little longer."

57

What Holds Me Back?

[Jesus] entered the synagogue, and a man was there who had a withered hand. They watched him to see whether he would cure him on the sabbath, so that they might accuse him. And he said to the man who had the withered hand, "Come forward." Then he said to them, "Is it lawful to do good or to do harm on the sabbath, to save life or to kill?" But they were silent. He looked around at them with anger; he was grieved at their hardness of heart and said to the man, "Stretch out your hand." He stretched it out, and his hand was restored. The Pharisees went out and immediately conspired with the Herodians against him, how to destroy him.

—Mark 3:1–6

Reflect

Jesus was being watched to see what he might do, yet it did not stop him from doing good, from restoring life. I ask God for the courage I need to do what I know is the right thing. Jesus teaches us that the great commandment is the law of love. Would people who know me be able to say that I follow the law of love?

Pray

Lord, when you celebrated the sabbath by healing a person, the Pharisees responded by plotting to kill you. You were showing that God does not want to make our lives more difficult and does not impose arbitrary rules on us. I let myself imagine how you want to brush away whatever it is that holds me back from living fully as God calls me to life. Please give me the strength I need to stretch out whatever ails me, in order to be healed.

58

Bad Times Are Not Evidence That God Is Punishing Me

At that very time there were some present who told him
about the Galileans whose blood Pilate had mingled with
their sacrifices. He asked them, "Do you think that because
these Galileans suffered in this way they were worse sinners
than all other Galileans? No, I tell you; but unless you repent,
you will all perish as they did. Or those eighteen who were
killed when the tower of Siloam fell on them—do you think
that they were worse offenders than all the others living in
Jerusalem? No, I tell you; but unless you repent, you will all
perish just as they did."

—Luke 13:1–5

Reflect

In Jesus' day there was a common belief that whatever misfortunes people experienced was a punishment for sin. The more a person suffered, the greater his or her sin must have been! Jesus rejected this simplistic notion. Instead he emphasized repentance, which means a turning toward God and toward one's neighbor. As always, Jesus tells us not only to look outward but also to look in; he is concerned with what is going on in our heads and in our hearts. He wants us to ask ourselves how God is opening us to compassion, prompting us to repentance, and leading us to life.

Pray

God, it's much easier to blame bad times on myself or others than to accept them as part of life and to work out how to get through them. Help me give up easy—and false—explanations. May I use these situations to go deeper in, to pray more, and to turn to you while extending compassion to others.

59

God Works Patiently with Me

Then he told this parable: "A man had a fig tree planted in his vineyard; and he came looking for fruit on it and found none. So he said to the gardener, 'See here! For three years I have come looking for fruit on this fig tree, and still I find none. Cut it down! Why should it be wasting the soil?' He replied, 'Sir, let it alone for one more year, until I dig around it and put manure on it. If it bears fruit next year, well and good; but if not, you can cut it down.'"

—Luke 13:6–9

Reflect

Cultivating and fertilizing the fig tree is a symbol of God's mercy in action. Divine love is patient, careful, gentle, and insistent. Can I see signs of this great care in my life right now?

Pray

Lord, you know my strengths and my frailties better than I do. You are a patient and loving God, and you have planted the seeds of change in my heart. Now is the time for these seeds to bear fruit. May I cooperate freely with your work in my life.

60

If Jesus Needed to Pray All Night . . .

Now during those days [Jesus] went out to the mountain to pray; and he spent the night in prayer to God. And when day came, he called his disciples and chose twelve of them, whom he also named apostles: Simon, whom he named Peter, and his brother Andrew, and James, and John, and Philip, and Bartholomew, and Matthew, and Thomas, and James son of Alphaeus, and Simon, who was called the Zealot, and Judas son of James, and Judas Iscariot, who became a traitor.

—Luke 6:12–16

Reflect

Jesus chose and called his disciples after some time of prayer. Consider what was in Jesus' heart: the hope, trust, and love he had for his disciples as he picked them to be close to him. Imagine what a night of prayer would feel like. Am I willing to spend that length of time talking to my heavenly Father?

Pray

Jesus, if you, the Son of God, needed long periods of prayer, then I surely need long periods of prayer sometimes, too. I don't know if I'm ready for that, but I'm willing to grow ready for it. Guide me on the way to a deeper life of prayer.

61

When Grieving the Loss of a Loved One

Early on the first day of the week, while it was still dark, Mary Magdalene came to the tomb and saw that the stone had been removed from the tomb. So she ran and went to Simon Peter and the other disciple, the one whom Jesus loved, and said to them, "They have taken the Lord out of the tomb, and we do not know where they have laid him." . . . Mary stood weeping outside the tomb. As she wept, she bent over to look into the tomb; and she saw two angels in white, sitting where the body of Jesus had been lying, one at the head and the other at the feet. They said to her, "Woman, why are you weeping?" She said to them, "They have taken away my Lord, and I do not know where they have laid him."

—John 20:1–2,11–13

Reflect

Mary weeps because she watched Jesus die and be laid in the tomb. She has already accepted that her loved one is gone. But now what? When you have lost a loved one, what does the world feel like for you? How do you feel, and how do you cope with that loss?

Pray

Lord, I know that in the verse that follows, Mary discovers that you have risen from the dead. But what can I do with the loss I have now? My loved one isn't going to rise from the dead today—as far as I know. You know when all these promises will come to pass, but I must live in the meantime. As far as I'm concerned, "They have taken my loved one away." Please bring comfort in these dark, difficult days.

62

When in Denial

Jesus said, "I came into this world for judgment so that those who do not see may see, and those who do see may become blind." Some of the Pharisees near him heard this and said to him, "Surely we are not blind, are we?" Jesus said to them, "If you were blind, you would not have sin. But now that you say, 'We see,' your sin remains."

—John 9:39–41

Reflect

Jesus is willing for everyone to encounter him and see the truth of the gospel. But he knows that not everyone truly wants to see. They are too attached to their own perceptions and ideas, and this makes them blind to whatever God may want to show them. This is true for everyone at one time or another. Is it true of me now? Are there any viewpoints or beliefs I'm too attached to?

Pray

Jesus, I think I want to see clearly, but it's possible that I am living in denial of some important truth about myself or about what God desires in my life. I'm willing to be made willing—to see, to understand, and to live out truth, mercy, and holiness.

63

I Need to Forgive, But It's So Hard to Do

Then Peter came and said to him, "Lord, if another member of the church sins against me, how often should I forgive? As many as seven times?" Jesus said to him, "Not seven times, but, I tell you, seventy-seven times."

—Matthew 18:21–22

Reflect

Jesus certainly understood human nature. He knew that Peter wanted a well-defined rule to follow, and to know when it was all right to give up on an offender. But Jesus said, in essence, that there should be no limit to our forgiveness. Perhaps he understood that sometimes we must forgive many times before we can let go of an offense. His guidance to Peter is for the person wronged as well as for the wrongdoer. The wrongdoer may need our patience, but our own grudge-keeping might require that we let go of blame, resentment, and anger multiple times.

Pray

Lord, it might take seventy-seven tries for me to let go of this hurt and anger because of what was done to me. It might take a hundred times. I want to let this go, and yet the feelings keep coming back. Help me forgive. Help me forgive, before this grudge eats away at my life and turns me into a hard, bitter person.

64

When I Want to Help Someone

Then the righteous will answer him, "Lord, when was it that we saw you hungry and gave you food, or thirsty and gave you something to drink? And when was it that we saw you a stranger and welcomed you, or naked and gave you clothing? And when was it that we saw you sick or in prison and visited you?" And the king will answer them, "Truly I tell you, just as you did it to one of the least of these who are members of my family, you did it to me."

—Matthew 25:37–40

Reflect

Sometimes we make things harder than they really are. We want to know how to support someone who is going through a difficult time. A card? A visit? It's very likely that the answer is right in front of us. What does this person need, truly? Help with housework? A friend to drive her to medical appointments? Company for lonely hours? Some extra food for the pantry? As we pray for those we want to help, we can also ask the Holy Spirit to guide us to the next step.

Pray

Holy Spirit, open my eyes, my ears, and my heart to what people around me are going through. Help me pay attention and take notice of what would help them. Show me the resources I have and how I might use them to love my neighbor.

65

Troubled Heart, Fearful Mind

"Do not let your hearts be troubled. Believe in God, believe also in me. In my Father's house there are many dwelling places. If it were not so, would I have told you that I go to prepare a place for you? And if I go and prepare a place for you, I will come again and will take you to myself, so that where I am, there you may be also. And you know the way to the place where I am going." Thomas said to him, "Lord, we do not know where you are going. How can we know the way?" Jesus said to him, "I am the way, and the truth, and the life. No one comes to the Father except through me. If you know me, you will know my Father also. From now on you do know him and have seen him."

—John 14:1–7

Reflect

Jesus speaks very plainly here. He prepares a place for us and will come for us so we can be with him. If we are confused by present circumstances, we can remember that Jesus, himself, is the way. As long as we are with him, we will find the right path, the right action, the right words. As we walk with Jesus, we can give up our troubled hearts and fearful minds. Can I believe this? Do I expect Jesus to meet me every day and show me the best way?

Pray

Show me who you are, Jesus, and where you are in my every day. Please hold on to me so that I don't stray from you. I want to be free from all those fears that can keep a person awake at night: fears about the future, about my decisions, about the resources I need. Bring me to a peaceful frame of mind and heart.

66

When Your Life Is at Its Bleakest Moment

Then Jesus went with them to a place called Gethsemane; and he said to his disciples, "Sit here while I go over there and pray." He took with him Peter and the two sons of Zebedee, and began to be grieved and agitated. Then he said to them, "I am deeply grieved, even to death; remain here, and stay awake with me." And going a little farther, he threw himself on the ground and prayed, "My Father, if it is possible, let this cup pass from me; yet not what I want but what you want." Then he came to the disciples and found them sleeping; and he said to Peter, "So, could you not stay awake with me one hour? Stay awake and pray that you may not come into the time of trial; the spirit indeed is willing, but the flesh is weak." Again he went away for the second time and prayed, "My Father, if this cannot pass unless I drink it, your will be done." Again he came and found them sleeping, for their eyes were heavy. So leaving them again, he went away and prayed for the third time, saying the same words. Then he came to the disciples and said to them, "Are you still sleeping and taking your rest? See, the hour is at hand, and the Son of Man is betrayed into the hands of sinners. Get up, let us be going. See, my betrayer is at hand."

—Matthew 26:36–46

Reflect

Jesus experienced that ultimate, bleak moment when he knew that everything was going to get much worse. He wanted to escape. He asked God to deliver him from all that was about to happen. And yet he wanted God's will no matter what. It's all right to want to escape from our bleakest moments. It's all right to ask God for deliverance—Jesus did. But our greatest freedom lies in that key part of his prayer: "your will be done." Can I pray those words now, in the midst of my dark, seemingly impossible problems? Can I face what happens next, knowing that it might be horrible? Can I be determined to follow God's leading?

Pray

I really want this situation to just stop, God. I'm not sure I can bear it anymore. But if I do what seems best, that means I stay where I am and deal with what comes next. If there's any way to do this differently, please show me. Otherwise, help me face my life with courage and hope.

67

Relationship Blame and Shame

Early in the morning he came again to the temple. All the people came to him and he sat down and began to teach them. The scribes and the Pharisees brought a woman who had been caught in adultery; and making her stand before all of them, they said to him, "Teacher, this woman was caught in the very act of committing adultery. Now in the law Moses commanded us to stone such women. Now what do you say?" They said this to test him, so that they might have some charge to bring against him. Jesus bent down and wrote with his finger on the ground. When they kept on questioning him, he straightened up and said to them, "Let anyone among you who is without sin be the first to throw a stone at her." And once again he bent down and wrote on the ground. When they heard it, they went away, one by one, beginning with the elders; and Jesus was left alone with the woman standing before him. Jesus straightened up and said to her, "Woman, where are they? Has no one condemned you?" She said, "No one, sir." And Jesus said, "Neither do I condemn you. Go your way, and from now on do not sin again."

—John 8:2–11

Reflect

In most places in the world today, adultery is not punishable by death as it was in Jesus' time. How do we look at this story, then? In place of that woman, can we see the person who has done damage to our relationship? Whether a boyfriend cheated, a close friend lied, or a family member cut ties with us, we have all suffered because of another person's actions. Who in my life might be this woman, found guilty? Or am I that person? Am I the one who bears the guilt and shame?

Pray

God, I know how it feels to heap guilt on someone. You know the relationship I'm thinking of. You know the hurt I've experienced, the betrayal. Like the woman in this story, the person is truly guilty, and I have a right to be angry. But I know that anger will not heal or help, not really. Grant me the freedom to relinquish the hate and condemnation that keep boiling inside me. Help me allow this person to go his or her way.

68

When I Need Wisdom and Discernment

[Jesus said to the disciples,] "When the Advocate comes, whom I will send to you from the Father, the Spirit of truth who comes from the Father, he will testify on my behalf. You also are to testify because you have been with me from the beginning.
"I have said these things to you to keep you from stumbling. They will put you out of the synagogues. Indeed, an hour is coming when those who kill you will think that by doing so they are offering worship to God. And they will do this because they have not known the Father or me. But I have said these things to you so that when their hour comes you may remember that I told you about them."
—John 15:26—16:4

Reflect

The work of the Holy Spirit, giving witness to what is true, affirms the life and love of Jesus. The Holy Spirit, the Counselor, does not operate as an alien intruder who whispers surprising news into my ear. Rather, the Holy Spirit helps me be myself and learn from my experience. I can discern where the Holy Spirit is working in my life. What evidence do I see of the Holy Spirit's work today?

Pray

Holy Spirit, you have come to guide me. I don't need to dread making decisions or figuring out what to do or not do. Help me pay attention to your work in my life. Help me to see God's gifts in the midst of my relationships and situations. Train me to reflect on my daily experience so that my insight can grow. Remind me of what Jesus has already taught me about how to live.

69

I Am So Weary

[Jesus said,] "Come to me, all you that are weary and are carrying heavy burdens, and I will give you rest. Take my yoke upon you, and learn from me; for I am gentle and humble in heart, and you will find rest for your souls. For my yoke is easy, and my burden is light."

—Matthew 11:28–30

Reflect

We become weary when life is too busy. We become burdened when we take on too many responsibilities. We become weary and burdened with the passing of years because we have carried so much grief, work, and effort. As time goes by, our bodies age and become weary, and their aches and ailments become burdens, too. Jesus asks that we take the life he offers because we will find rest in his presence. How can I bring my fatigue and burdens to him now?

Pray

I am often weary, Lord, and my burden feels heavy. And I confess that, at times, I feel at war with aging and all that it means for my physical life. I know that some of my body's pains are probably related to anxiety and all the pressure I put on myself. Show me how to work alongside you and take on your gentle, humble outlook. Free me of burdens I shouldn't even have. May I be at peace in my physical life. But most of all, may I be at peace in my soul.

70

Overwhelmed with Worries

"Therefore I tell you, do not worry about your life, what you will eat or what you will drink, or about your body, what you will wear. Is not life more than food, and the body more than clothing? Look at the birds of the air; they neither sow nor reap nor gather into barns, and yet your heavenly Father feeds them. Are you not of more value than they? And can any of you by worrying add a single hour to your span of life? And why do you worry about clothing? Consider the lilies of the field, how they grow; they neither toil nor spin, yet I tell you, even Solomon in all his glory was not clothed like one of these. But if God so clothes the grass of the field, which is alive today and tomorrow is thrown into the oven, will he not much more clothe you—you of little faith? Therefore do not worry, saying, "What will we eat?" or "What will we drink?" or "What will we wear?" For it is the Gentiles who strive for all these things; and indeed your heavenly Father knows that you need all these things. But strive first for the kingdom of God and his righteousness, and all these things will be given to you as well.

"So do not worry about tomorrow, for tomorrow will bring worries of its own. Today's trouble is enough for today."

—Matthew 6:25–34

Reflect

Do I dare to take Jesus seriously when he says not to worry about food and clothing—not to worry about my life? He paints a picture of a world in which God's care sustains every single living thing, from flowers and birds to people, in all their complexity. It is useless to pile up tomorrow's worries on top of today's—and yet how much of my anxiety has to do with the future? Is there even one worry I can release this day?

Pray

God of all bounty, I tend to think of this world as a place of scarcity and want. And this kind of thinking makes me afraid for tomorrow. I want to see your presence in my life. I want to be aware of the gifts you offer. Please deliver me from constant worry and fear. Jesus wants me to be free and joyful, and that's what I want, too.

About the Editor

Vinita Hampton Wright has edited books on Ignatian spirituality for nineteen years and writes regularly for LoyolaPress.com and Ignatianspirituality.com. She is the author of numerous books, including *Days of Deepening Friendship* and *The Art of Spiritual Writing*. Wright is the managing editor of trade books at Loyola Press and lives in Chicago with her husband.